MASTERING NEW YORK'S GRADE 3 READING STANDARDS:
Student Activities

MARK JARRETT   **STUART ZIMMER**   **JAMES KILLORAN**
Ph.D., Stanford University

CARROLL MOULTON   **WILLIAM REDMOND**
Ph.D., Yale University

JARRETT PUBLISHING COMPANY

EAST COAST OFFICE
P.O. Box 1460
Ronkonkoma, NY 11779
631-981-4248

SOUTHERN OFFICE
50 Nettles Boulevard
Jensen Beach, FL 34957
800-859-7679

WEST COAST OFFICE
10 Folin Lane
Lafayette, CA 94549
925-906-9742

www.jarrettpub.com
1-800-859-7679   Fax: 631-588-4722

Jarrett Publishing Company
Post Office Box 1460
Ronkonkoma, New York 11779

ISBN 1-9795493-4-5 [978-0-9795493-4-2]
Printed in the United States of America
First Edition
10 9 8 7 6 5 4 3 2 1   10 09 08 07

INTRODUCTION

This activity book is designed to be used with *Mastering New York's Grade 3 English Language Arts Standards*. Unlike that book, this one does not contain definitions, step-by-step explanations, or multiple-choice questions except in the practice final found in the last chapter.

Instead, this activity book provides additional readings and exercises to reinforce what you will learn in *Mastering New York's Grade 3 English Language Arts Standards*. The activities in this book will help you master the vocabulary and reading comprehension skills you need to improve your performance on the **New York Grade 3 English Language Arts Test**.

How can you use these books together? After completing each chapter in *Mastering New York's Grade 3 English Language Arts Standards*, you should turn to the activities in the companion chapter of this book. Your teacher may want to complete the activities in this book before answering the questions in the "Now You Try It" sections at the end of each chapter of *Mastering New York's Grade 3 English Language Arts Standards*.

Name ______________________________ Date ____________

HOW TO BE A GOOD READER

Directions. The following chart shows seven methods you can use to be a good reader. Fill in the chart to tell about each method that good readers use. The first one has been done for you.

Ask Yourself Questions
Good readers ask questions about what they are reading.

Make Connections

____

____

____

Think about What's Important

____

____

____

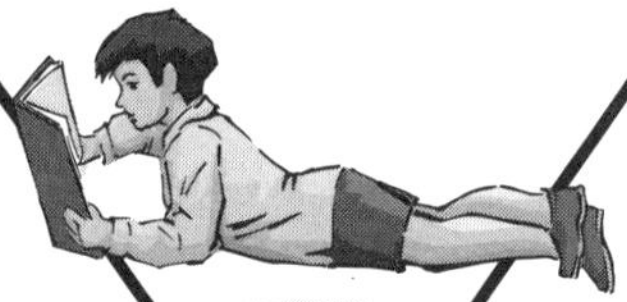

Methods Used By Good Readers

Summarize

____

____

____

____

Make Predictions

____

____

____

____

Create Mental Images

____

____

____

Be a Problem-Solver

____

____

____

Name _____   Date _____

Directions. Read the following article about windmills. In the spaces alongside these paragraphs, use the methods of good readers.

MAKE CONNECTIONS

From the title, what connections can you make to what you already know?

_____

_____

MAKE PREDICTIONS

What do you predict the article will be about?

_____

_____

CREATE MENTAL IMAGES

From these details, what mental images can you create?

_____

_____

BE A PROBLEM SOLVER

Do you know what a windmill is? If not, how would you find out?

_____

_____

WINDMILLS FIXED THE FLOODS

by Carmen Bredeson

Hundreds of years ago, nearly half of Holland was covered with water. Much of the land was below sea level and was often flooded by the North Sea. This made the land swampy.

Dutch people needed the land for farming. They began building dikes, which are huge walls of dirt. Dikes held back water from the North Sea. But farmers also needed a way to pump out the water that was already on the land.

Windmills were the answer. For hundreds of years, windmills had been in use all over the world. Some windmills ground grain into flour. Others sawed logs into lumber. During the 1400s and 1500s, the Dutch built windmills to pump water from the land. Luckily for them, Holland is very windy.

Name _____ Date _____

ASK QUESTIONS

What questions do you have about windmills?

_____

_____

_____

THINK ABOUT
WHAT IS IMPORTANT

Starting in the 1800s, what happened to many of the windmills?

_____

_____

_____

_____

SUMMARIZE

How would you summarize this last paragraph?

_____

_____

_____

_____

_____

_____

Thanks to windmills, fields that were once under water were now dry. They could be used for crops. The drained fields were called *polders*. Storms and floods brought more water to the land. Windmills kept turning to keep the fields dry.

In the 1800s, steam engines and electricity started powering the pumps that drained the fields. The new pumps could work even when it was not windy. Many of the old windmills were torn down. Hundreds more were burned or destroyed in storms. Lightning struck many of the old wooden windmills because they were the tallest things in the fields.

Holland once had nearly 10,000 windmills. Today only about 900 are left. Special organizations are trying to save the windmills. Many are kept in working order. In case the modern pumps fail, the old windmills could be used again. Wind-mills remain an important part of the history and landscape of Holland.

● ACTIVITY A

Directions. Pick five vocabulary words from the article, "Windmills Fixed the Floods." Look up the meaning of each word in a dictionary. On the lines below, write each vocabulary word. Then use each word in a sentence of your own.

	Word	Use the Word in a Sentence
1.		
2.		
3.		
4.		
5.		

● ACTIVITY B

Choose one detail or scene described in the reading passage. In the space provided below, draw a picture to illustrate that detail or scene.

Name _____   Date _____

ACTIVITY C

Directions. Suppose you wanted to find out how windmills are used today in different parts of the world. Think about the information you learned from this article about windmills in Holland. Then write four questions that could guide your research about windmills around the world. You may want work in small groups to research your questions on-line.

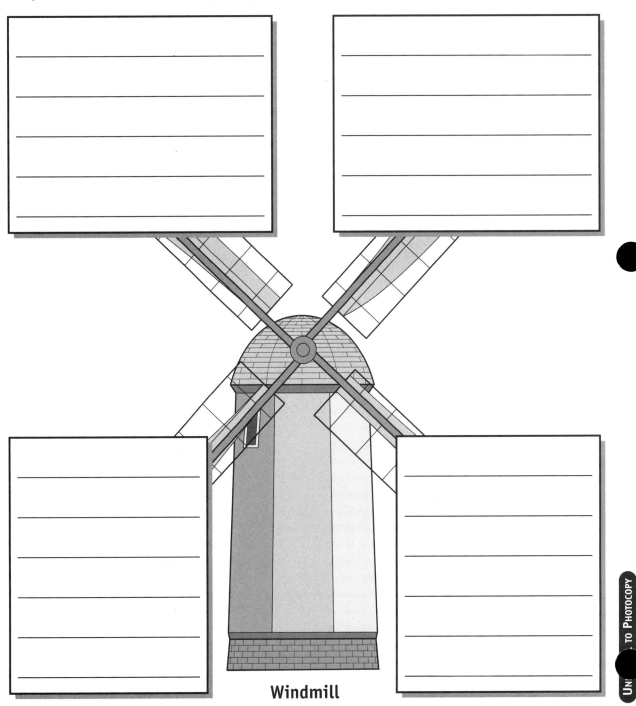

Windmill

● ACTIVITY D

Directions. On page 4, you wrote a summary of the last paragraph of the article. In the space below, write a summary of the whole article. Remember, a good summary gives the most important ideas of the reading passage in your own words.

SHOWING INFORMATION
IN DIFFERENT WAYS

Directions. Read the story "Ostrich and Crocodile" below. Then complete the exercises that follow.

The Sesotho people live in southern Africa. They tell this story about how Ostrich got his long neck.

OSTRICH AND CROCODILE

Long ago, Ostrich was like most other birds. His neck was not very long in those days, Ostrich and Crocodile were very good friends. The other animals were afraid of crocodiles. They warned Ostrich. "Stay away from Crocodile," they told him. "Don't trust him." But Ostrich paid no attention. He felt sorry that Crocodile had so few friends.

One morning, Crocodile woke up feeling very hungry. He had not eaten for a long time. The other animals were afraid to go near him. Crocodile might grab them and pull them into the water. Then he would have his meal.

But Ostrich walked on his long feet right up to the water. Crocodile said to him, "Welcome, my dear friend! Maybe you can help me. You know how many teeth I have. I am always having trouble with one tooth or another. Right now, one of my back teeth on the left side is aching badly. The pain is terrible. Please put your head inside my mouth. You might be able to find the painful tooth."

Crocodile opened his strong jaws wide. Ostrich did not suspect a trick. So he put his head into Crocodile's large mouth.

Then Crocodile quickly closed his jaws. He started to pull Ostrich into the water.

Now Ostrich knew he had been fooled. He was strong, though. He started to pull backward in the other direction. He knew he had to get away from the water.

Ostrich and Crocodile both pulled and pulled. Ostrich's neck began to stretch. It stretched and stretched. Ostrich did not give in. His neck got longer and longer.

Finally, Crocodile gave up. He was tired from the struggle. He opened his jaws, and Ostrich escaped. Ever since then, Ostrich has kept his long neck. He lives in dry places, away from water. And he never talks to crocodiles.

ACTIVITY A

Directions. Use details from the passage to fill out the *web* or *cluster* below for the character of Crocodile in the story. One of the details about Crocodile has been filled in for you.

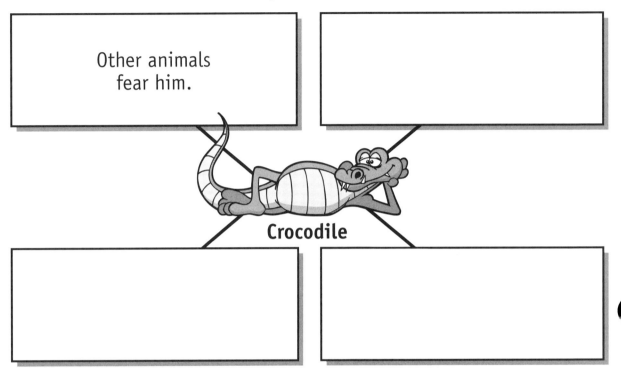

Other animals fear him.

Crocodile

ACTIVITY B

Directions. Fill in the *Venn diagram* below to show how Ostrich and Crocodile are like each other and how they are different. Notice that part of the diagram has been filled in for you.

Ostrich
lives in dry places

★ _____
★ _____
★ _____

Both
friends long ago

★ _____
★ _____
★ _____

Crocodile
has many teeth

★ _____
★ _____
★ _____

● ACTIVITY C

Directions. Use events from the story to complete the *sequence map* shown below. The first few entries have been done for you.

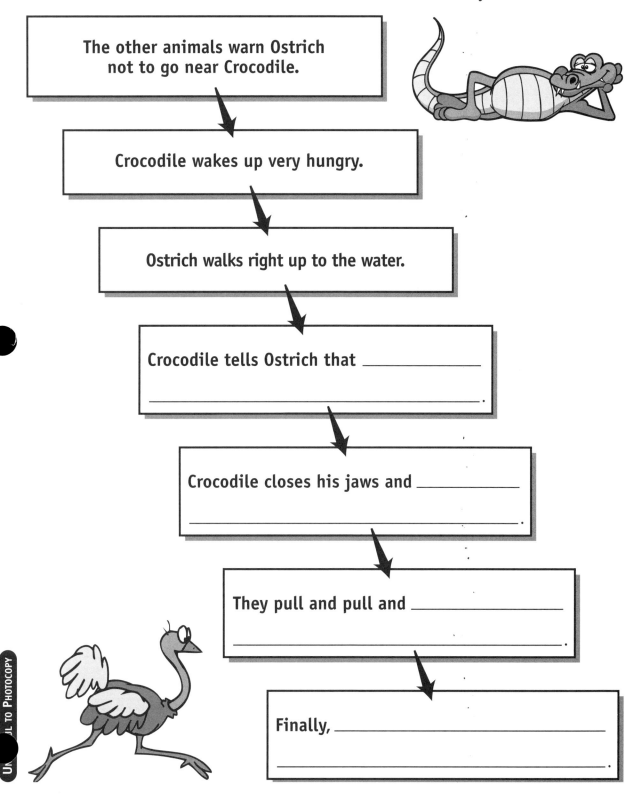

The other animals warn Ostrich not to go near Crocodile.

Crocodile wakes up very hungry.

Ostrich walks right up to the water.

Crocodile tells Ostrich that _____ _____ .

Crocodile closes his jaws and _____ _____ .

They pull and pull and _____ _____ .

Finally, _____ _____ .

READING LITERATURE

THE PARTS OF A STORY

ACTIVITY A

Directions. For each numbered item in Column A, choose the correct definition from Column B. Write the matching letters on the lines in Column A.

Column A	Column B
1. ___ Setting	**a.** what happens in a story
2. ___ Characters	**b.** the message or lesson of a story
3. ___ Plot	**c.** when and where a story takes place
4. ___ Theme	**d.** who the story is about

Directions. Read the story, "My Sister Snores." Then complete the activities that follow.

MY SISTER SNORES
by Shannon Hitchcock

My sister snores. Sometimes Emily sounds as if she's blowing her nose. Other times she sounds like a train whistle. *Snort, sniff, snuffle, uuuggchooo, uuggchooo!* Last night was the loudest night ever. I tried sleeping with my earmuffs on, but they weren't very comfortable.

I thought about my problem all day. At dinner I asked my mom, "May I move into the guest room? Emily snores so much that I can't sleep." "I do not snore," Emily said. "But I would love having my own room. Jessica is messy."

Mom said, "We'll give it a try. Jessica can sleep in the guest room tonight." We raced up the stairs to our room. I said to Emily, "I am not messy." Emily raised her eyebrows and looked around the room. She patted my lumpy bed. She picked up my pajamas from the floor, and peered at the toys stuffed under my bed. "Face it, Jess, you're messy."

"Well, I would rather be messy than snore." I stomped out of our room. At eight o'clock, Mom tucked me into bed. Later, I heard a loud rumbling noise. "Mom, what's that scary sound?" I called.

"It's only the furnace," she answered. It's funny that I never heard the furnace when I was sleeping with Emily. My new room was as dark as a dungeon, even with the night-light. I stared at the closet door. I wondered what scary things were hiding in there. "Mom, how long have I been sleeping in my new room?" I called.

"One hour," she answered.

I still had nine more hours until morning. Nine hours seemed like forever. I thought about Emily. There were a lot of good things about sharing a room with my sister. She would say, "It's not real," when I had a bad dream. And we always whispered secrets late at night.

I looked up and saw Emily standing in the doorway. She said, "I came to borrow your earmuffs. You're yelling so much that I can't sleep." I whispered, "I'm a tiny bit scared. Just for tonight, will you sleep with me in my new room?"

"OK," she said.

I raised the covers and Emily climbed in. She handed me my ear-muffs from the bedside table. "Just in case," she said.

I laughed. I love Emily — even when she snores.

ACTIVITY B

Directions. Briefly describe the story **setting** in "My Sister Snores." Fill in the chart below.

"MY SISTER SNORES": THE SETTING	
When	**Where**
_____	_____
_____	_____

ACTIVITY C

Directions. Who are the three **characters** in the story? Identify the characters on the lines below.

Character 1:	
Character 2:	
Character 3:	

ACTIVITY D

Directions. In the lines provided, answer the following questions about the **plot** of the story.

1. What problems do the main characters face? _____

_____

_____

2. What actions do the characters take to deal with these problems?

_____

_____

3. How are these problems finally solved? _____

_____

_____

ACTIVITY E

Directions. Answer the following questions about the **theme** of the story "My Sister Snores."

What is the message of this story? _____

_____

_____

_____

_____

Does the theme of the story remind you of anything that has happened in your own life or that you have learned about? Explain.

_____

_____

_____

_____

POEMS

ACTIVITY F

Directions. For each numbered item in Column A, choose the correct definition shown in Column B. Write the matching letters on the lines provided.

Column A	Column B
1. ___ Rhythm	**a.** a paragraph of several lines in a poem
2. ___ Rhyme	**b.** the beat of the lines in a poem
3. ___ Stanza	**c.** word pictures that appeal to the senses
4. ___ Imagery	**d.** a similar last sound is repeated

Directions. Read the poem "February Twilight." Then complete the activities that follow.

FEBRUARY TWILIGHT
by Sara Teasdale

1 I stood beside a hill
2 Smooth with new-laid snow,
3 A single star looked out
4 From the cold evening glow.

5 There was no other creature
6 That saw what I could see —
7 I stood and watched the evening star
8 As long as it watched me.

⬤ACTIVITY G

Directions. Check your understanding of the poem "February Twilight" by answering the following questions.

1. What is the poem mostly about? _____

   _____

   _____

2. How many stanzas are in the poem? [   ]

3. Which words in the poem rhyme? Identify all of the rhyming words by line number.

Rhyming Word	Line Number
_____ **and** _____	_____
_____ **and** _____	_____

4. What two senses does the imagery in the poem appeal to?

    ★ _____   ★ _____

   Explain your answers. _____

   _____

   _____

   _____

   _____

5. How does the poet feel about the twilight (early evening)? _____

_____

_____

_____

_____

_____

6. Why do you think the poet feels this way? _____

_____

_____

_____

_____

_____

_____

_____

_____

_____

READING FOR INFORMATION

ACTIVITY A

Directions. For each numbered item in Column A, choose the correct definition from Column B. Write the matching letters on the lines provided.

Column A	Column B
1. ___ Article	**a.** tells about an author's own life
2. ___ Essay	**b.** tells about another person's life
3. ___ Biography	**c.** gives the basic facts about something
4. ___ Autobiography	**d.** gives an author's feelings on a topic

Directions. Now read the informational article "A Special Group of People." Then complete the activities that follow.

A SPECIAL GROUP OF PEOPLE
by Carroll Moulton

All through our history, the First Ladies of America have been a very special group of people. The title "First Lady" was not used for the President's wife until the mid-1800s. Long before that, though, the First Lady played an important part in the history of the United States.

Martha Washington was the first "First Lady." She was famous long before her husband George Washington became the first President. During the American Revolutionary War, George Washington was the Commander-in-Chief of the Continental Army. Martha Washington made many trips to stay with her husband in camp. She often risked her own safety to heal the sick, mend clothing, and cook food for the soldiers.

Martha Washington

Roads were bad in those days. The winter weather was very cold. Travel was hard, even for short distances. Martha Washington still had a strong desire to support her husband and his troops. The public called Martha, "Lady Washington." She had no model for her role. Instead, she became a model for future First Ladies.

Dolley Madison was the wife of the fourth President, James Madison. Dolley was known for her warmth and charm. Her parties, called "receptions" or "crushes," were the talk of Washington.

Dolley Madison

Dolley was also brave and strong. During the War of 1812, British soldiers burned and looted Washington. Dolley saved valuable papers and portraits. She took them from a burning White House and kept them safe until the war was over.

Eleanor Roosevelt was the wife of Franklin Delano Roosevelt, our 32nd President. When she was young, Eleanor was quiet and shy. But after Franklin came down with polio, Eleanor served as his eyes and ears.

Eleanor traveled all over the United States to find out what people were thinking and feeling. She was a talented writer and speaker. She worked hard for many social causes and for human rights.

Eleanor Roosevelt

Lady Bird Johnson

In more recent times, First Ladies have often chosen an area to work on with special energy. Lady Bird Johnson, for example, focused on the environment. Today, the Lady Bird Johnson Wildflower Center in Austin, Texas, carries out valuable research on plants and wildflowers.

Laura Bush, the wife of President George W. Bush, also comes from Texas. Laura once worked as a teacher. She earned a degree in library science. Laura's special area is education and reading. She has taken her place in a long line of remarkable people: the First Ladies of our land.

Laura Bush

ACTIVITY B

Directions. Identify the topic, the main idea, and one supporting detail from the article "A Special Group of People."

★ **Topic:** _____

_____

_____

_____

★ **Main Idea:** _____

_____

_____

_____

★ **One Detail:** _____

_____

_____

_____

ACTIVITY C

Directions. Check your understanding of the article "A Special Group of People" by answering the following questions.

1. What details are used by the writer to show that Martha Washington was brave and strong? _____

_____

_____

2. Why do you think the writer includes Dolley Madison in this article?

_____

_____

Name _____ Date _____

● **3.** What details does the writer use to show that Eleanor Roosevelt was a special First Lady? _____

_____

_____

_____

4. Which two First Ladies from recent times are discussed in the article?

★ _____   ★ _____

5. For each of the two First Ladies you just named, identify a special interest or area of activity.

★ _____

● _____

★ _____

_____

6. How does the author feel about the First Ladies? _____ _____

_____

_____

_____

7. Which details from the article led you to this conclusion?

_____

● _____

_____

WORD-MEANING QUESTIONS

ACTIVITY A

Directions. Read each numbered item below. Then answer the questions that follow each sentence.

---

1. The elevator quickly **ascended** from the building lobby to the 40th floor, where the apartments had a beautiful view.

   ★ What is the meaning of "ascended"?

   _____

   ★ What clue helped you figure out the meaning? _____

   _____

---

2. The train passed through a **rural** area, where farms stretched out as far as the eye could see.

   ★ What is the meaning of "rural"? _____

   ★ What clue helped you figure out the meaning? _____

---

3. Unlike today's small personal computers, the computers of the 1970s were **massive**.

   ★ What is the meaning of "massive"?

   _____

   ★ What clue helped you figure out the meaning? _____

   _____

Name _____ Date _____

⬤ **4.** We woke up at **daybreak**, when light was beginning to glow in the eastern sky.

★ What is the meaning of "daybreak"? _____

★ What clue helped you figure out the meaning? _____

_____

---

5. Jack lived in an **urban** environment in the center of a large city.

★ What is the meaning of "urban"?

_____

★ What clue helped you figure out the meaning? _____

_____

⬤ **6.** As it **lurched** from side to side in the stormy weather, the boat became very difficult to control.

★ What is the meaning of 'lurched"? _____

★ What clues helped you figure out the meaning? _____

_____

---

7. Emily's new business quickly became a great **success**, and she had to hire three more people to handle all the orders.

★ What is the meaning of "success"?

_____

★ What clue helped you figure out the meaning? _____

_____

8. Many animals **protect** themselves in special ways. For example, some animals use their color to help keep themselves safe.

★ What is the meaning of "protect"? _____

_____

★ What clue helped you figure out the meaning? _____

_____

_____

---

9. The roots and history of our town, or its **heritage**, was the theme of the museum exhibits.

★ What is the meaning of "heritage"? _____

_____

★ What clues helped you figure out the meaning? _____

_____

ACTIVITY B

Directions. Use prefixes, root words, and suffixes from the jars below to build seven words of your own.

Prefixes

in-   mis-   un-   pre-   dis-   re-

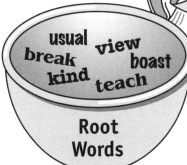

Root Words

usual   view   break   boast   kind   teach

Suffixes

-able   -ful   -ness   -er   -ing   -ed

Write the words you create on the lines below. Check your words in a dictionary. Be prepared to explain their definitions.

1. _____

2. _____

3. _____

4. _____

5. _____

6. _____

7. _____

ACTIVITY C

Directions. Read each paragraph below. Use context and word analysis clues to figure out the meaning of the words in dark type. Write the meaning of each word in the space provided.

In Chicago, the summer and fall of 1871 were very dry. It had not rained for many months. Because of the **drought**, dry wooden buildings, lumber yards and grain storehouses were ready to catch fire.

★ **drought:** _____

Many people have wondered what makes the oceans rise and fall on the world's beaches twice a day. These tides are caused by the force of the moon's **gravity** and the **rotation** of the Earth as it turns on its axis.

★ **gravity:** _____

★ **rotation:** _____

The invention of the telescope in the early 1600s was a **milestone** in the history of science. Telescopes **magnified** distant objects in the night sky. and allowed **astronomers** to observe them closely. Using a telescope, the Italian scientist Galileo discovered four of the moons of Jupiter.

★ **milestone:** _____

★ **magnified:** _____

★ **astronomers:** _____

The next day, Tashira **strolled** slowly over to the park. The swings were empty. A gang of boys was scaring little children away. Then Officer Hamlette came along. When the bad boys saw him, they became **alarmed** and ran off. Officer Hamlette stood on the corner. He watched the boys go. Before long, all the little children **emerged** from their hiding places. They began to play on the swings.

★ **strolled:** _____

★ **alarmed:** _____

★ **emerged:** _____

ACTIVITY D

Directions. In each sentence, pay special attention to words in dark type. Use context and word analysis clues to figure out the meaning of each word. Then fill in the blank with a **synonym** or **antonym** for that word.

1. If you look at a map of the United States, you will see that rivers often form the **frontiers** between states.

   Synonym: _____

Name _____   Date _____

2. During World War II, the United States was an **ally** to England, France, and Russia. These four countries fought together against Germany, Japan, and Italy.

Antonym: _____

3. The performers in the cast of a play are always thrilled when spectators **applaud** their performances.

Synonym: _____

4. Unfortunately, the vase fell off the table and **smashed** into many tiny pieces.

Synonym: _____

5. The crowds attending the parade were **jubilant** when they caught sight of the marching bands and the enormous floats.

Antonym: _____

6. Mom prepared lunch **hurriedly** because she had to attend a special meeting at the library.

Antonym: _____

7. Jamal knew the facts of the case extremely well, and his answers to the judge's questions were detailed and **precise**.

Synonym: _____

8. The editor asked the writer to **simplify** her article to make it easier to read.

Synonym: _____

9. Leonardo da Vinci, a famous writer, scientist, painter, and engineer, had a **remarkable** career.

Antonym: _____

10. It was clear from his sarcastic, disrespectful comments that he intended to **mock** us.

Synonym: _____

11. Everyone wore **casual** clothes to the party, which took place outdoors around a BBQ grill near the swimming pool.

Antonym: _____

12. The business did so well that its owners decided to **expand** their warehouse space so that more products could be stored there.

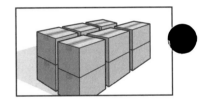

Antonym: _____

13. The defense attorney asked the judge to treat her client with **compassion**, but the judge sentenced the convicted thief to jail.

Synonym: _____

14. When still young, deer learn to **avoid** animals like wolves, which threaten them.

Synonym: _____

15. "You need to **grasp** the bat firmly and keep your eye on the ball," my baseball coach told me.

Synonym: _____

UNDERSTANDING THE BIG PICTURE

Directions. Read the Aesop fable below. Then answer the questions.

THE FOX AND THE CROW

Crows are hungry most of the time. They often steal food from other birds, animals, and people. One day, a crow stole a piece of cheese from a farmer. He flew to the top of a tall pine tree. "I will perch here," he said to himself. "The view from this tree is wonderful. It is a good place for me to enjoy my meal."

Now it happened that a fox walked up and stopped under the same tree. He saw the crow, black as ink, sitting on a high branch. He also saw the cheese in the bird's beak. "Let me see about this," the fox thought. "Maybe I will have cheese tonight for dinner."

The fox sat under the tree patiently. After some time, he spoke to the crow in a polite and very friendly way.

"Good afternoon, Sir Crow! My, how handsome you are looking today! Your wings are shining with good health. You look as strong as an eagle! You have such powerful claws."

The crow looked down at the fox in surprise. The compliments the fox had paid him made him feel very pleased.

"But what about your voice?" asked the fox. "Crows are well known for their calls. I'm sure your voice is splendid. When you sing, how the other birds must envy you!"

The crow puffed out his wings and wagged his tail to show his pleasure. No one had ever called his "caw" sounds beautiful before. Without thinking, he opened his mouth to sing.

The cheese dropped straight to the ground. The clever fox quickly snatched it up. Before he left to enjoy his dinner, the fox spoke to the crow one last time.

"Be careful when someone praises you. Flatterers are not to be trusted."

1. What is the main conflict in the story? _____

_____

_____

2. How do the characters resolve this conflict? _____

_____

_____

3. Write a **single sentence** that summarizes what the story is mostly about. _____

_____

Name _____ Date _____

Directions. Now read the poem "The Bat." After you finish reading, answer the questions that follow.

THE BAT
by Theodore Roethke

By day the bat is cousin to the mouse.
He likes the attic of an aging house.

His fingers make a hat above his head.
His pulse beat is so slow we think him dead.

He loops in crazy figures half the night.
Among the trees that face the corner light.

But when he brushes up against a screen,
We are afraid of what our eyes have seen:

For something is amiss or out of place
When mice with wings can wear a human face.

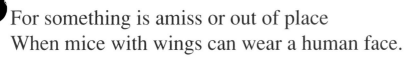

1. Does the poem tell a story or does it describe the speaker's feelings about something? Put a check mark in one of the boxes below.

   ☐ Tells a story   ☐ Describes feelings

2. What is the topic of the poem? _____

   _____

3. How does the speaker feel about the topic? How do you know?

   _____

   _____

   _____

Name _____   Date _____

Directions. Now read the informational article "Our Robot Helpers" shown below. Then answer the questions that follow.

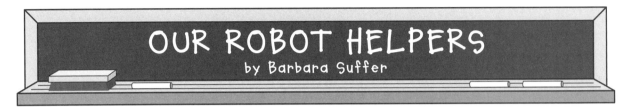

OUR ROBOT HELPERS
by Barbara Suffer

You may not realize it, but robots are an important part of your life. They make the televisions you watch, the cars you ride in, and the video games you play. Some robots help doctors perform brain surgery, while others bring meals to hospital patients. Robots are especially useful for performing dangerous jobs — like repairing power plants or disarming a bomb.

Most people think of robots as machines that look more or less like humans. In real life, however, most robots do not look like people at all.

Robots are machines run by computers. Most look like boxes or tubes with one or more "arms" that do some job, such as packing oranges or painting cars. Some robots have tracks, wheels, or legs so they can explore the ocean floor or carry out other jobs.

There is, of course, a big difference between robots and humans. Robots can't think or create new ideas. One day, however, this may change. Scientists are trying to make robots with the ability to learn, think, and solve problems like people do.

Someday robots may learn to think and act like humans. Will they then be human? Many scientists don't think so. They believe the human ability to feel pleasure, pain, joy, and sadness cannot be created in a machine. No matter how smart robots become, they are unlikely ever to develop human feelings.

34

1. What is the topic of this article? _____

   _____

2. What does the author say about this topic? _____

   _____

   _____

   _____

3. Write **one sentence** that summarizes the main idea of the article. _____

   _____

   _____

   _____

4. Now write a **summary** of the article in one paragraph.

   _____

   _____

   _____

   _____

   _____

   _____

   _____

LOOKING AT THE DETAILS

Directions. Read the informational article "Monument Valley: Past and Present." Then answer the questions that follow.

MONUMENT VALLEY: PAST AND PRESENT

The desert is an ever-changing place. Some 250 million years ago, giant sand dunes covered the southwestern United States. This area today includes the states of Nevada, Utah, Colorado, New Mexico, and Arizona.

To the east, wind and water wore away a great mountain chain. Bits of rock from these mountains swept westward. The rock added new layers of sand to the desert. In time, this sand hardened into sandstone.

Millions of years passed. Seas washed across the land and then retreated. Erosion again shaped the land. In some spots, the sandstone was protected by flat caps of harder rock. The sandstone underneath each cap remained. But in most cases, wind and water swept away the land, carving fantastic forms out of the red sandstone.

Name _____   Date _____

Today these forms make up the best-known landscape in the West — the spires, buttes, and mesas of Monument Valley. A spire is a tall, circular shape with a sharp point, while a butte is a steep hill standing alone on a plain. A mesa is an area of flat tableland with steep sides.

Long ago, Monument Valley must have been a very lonely place. Even today, the landscape has a bare, plain look. Nevertheless, many tourists come every year to see Monument Valley. The area is part of a tribal park belonging to the Navajo Indians. During the peak tourist season, from May to October, tourists fill the hotels and motels near Monument Valley. Visitors drive through the park on a 17-mile dirt road. On the rim of the valley, there is a visitor center which includes a restaurant.

Today, Monument Valley is one of the best-known places in the West because it has been featured in many films and television shows. In the movie *2001: A Space Odyssey*, made in 1968, the valley was used for scenes set on a different planet. In the movie *The Eiger Sanction* (1975), actor Clint Eastwood was shown on top of a spire in the valley called the "Totem Pole." In *Mission Impossible II*, actor Tom Cruise is filmed climbing in Monument Valley. Because Monument Valley stands as a symbol of the Old West in American history, many Westerns have also been filmed there.

Poster from
Mission Impossible II

Name _____   Date _____

ACTIVITY A

Directions. Practice your skill at scanning by completing a "treasure hunt" for details in the article. Fill in the blank for each item below.

1. Sand dunes covered the southwestern United States _____ years ago.

2. Three states in this region are Nevada, Utah, and _____.

3. After bits of rock and sand swept westward, they hardened here into

   _____.

4. The most important process that shaped the land in this area is called

   _____.

5. Three of the fantastic forms carved in Monument Valley are spires, buttes, and _____.

6. Today, Monument Valley is part of a tribal park that belongs to the _____ Indians.

7. The peak tourist season in Monument Valley is from

   _____ to _____.

8. One of the films made in Monument Valley was

   _____.

9. *Mission Impossible II*, with a scene in Monument Valley, starred the actor _____.

10. Monument Valley remains a symbol of _____ in American history.

● ACTIVITY B

Directions. Complete the sequence map with events mentioned in the article. Put the events in time order on the map.

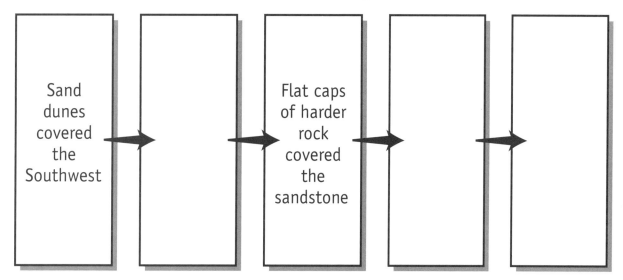

● ACTIVITY C

Directions. Use details from the article to fill in the cause-and-effect charts shown below.

1.

Cause	Effect
Flat caps protected the sandstone.	

2.

Cause	Effect
Wind and water swept across the land.	

3.

Cause		Effect
	→	The sand hardened into sandstone.

4.

Cause		Effect
	→	Many Westerns have been filmed in Monument Valley.

ACTIVITY D

Directions. Use the Venn diagram below to compare Monument Valley long ago with how it is now. On the left-hand side, give details about Monument Valley long ago. On the right-hand side, give details about Monument Valley now. In the overlapping area on the diagram, list details that are similar to both.

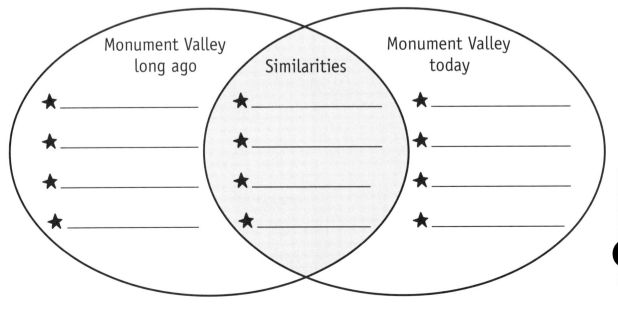

Monument Valley long ago
★ _____
★ _____
★ _____
★ _____

Similarities
★ _____
★ _____
★ _____
★ _____

Monument Valley today
★ _____
★ _____
★ _____
★ _____

Name _____   Date _____

⬤ACTIVITY E

Directions. Answer the following questions about the main idea and the supporting details in the article.

1. Write a single sentence stating the main idea of the article "Monument Valley: Past and Present."

   _____

   _____

   _____

   _____

2. Write **three details** from the article that support the main idea.

   ★ _____

   _____

   _____

   ★ _____

   _____

   _____

   ★ _____

   _____

   _____

QUESTIONS ABOUT STORIES

Directions. Read the story "Jared to the Rescue." Then complete the exercises that follow.

JARED TO THE RESCUE
by Carole Duncan Buckman

On the first morning of third grade, Jared remembered five things he didn't like about school: Jessica, lining up, arithmetic, spelling, and reading aloud. Jared wanted to stay home, but his mom sent him anyway. He had to sit next to Jessica.

At reading time, Mrs. Thomas asked Jared to read. Reading aloud made Jared nervous. As he picked up the book, his hands shook. Words blurred. "He can't read," Jessica shouted out.

"I didn't call on you, did I?" said Mrs. Thomas to Jessica.

"No, but I'll read," replied Jessica.

Jared made a face. Both Jared and Jessica were punished by being sent to time-out. Jessica whispered to Jared, "When Mom brings my kittens to school, don't even think about touching them."

The four kittens arrived in a box covered with a piece of screen. Everyone but Jared held them. Jared practiced spelling. When he sharpened his pencil, he peeked into the box. "Don't touch my kittens!" Jessica hissed.

After show-and-tell, the children took out their arithmetic books. Then Philip shouted, "Hey, where are the kittens?" The box was empty!

"Oh no!" Jessica said. "Jared, did you take them?"

Jared shook his head. "They must have pushed up the lid."

"Look at the radiator!" Angela said. Tiny gray paws pushed out from under the radiator cover.

"Kitty, kitty," Mrs. Thomas said. The paws disappeared. "If we ignore them, maybe they'll come out. At least the heat isn't on."

Instead of adding and subtracting, Jared watched the radiator. Soon, two paws and a tiny head appeared. Alex yelled, "Kitten!" The kitten zipped back out of sight. Jessica cried. Jared gave her a tissue.

A bell rang, and the class filed out for recess. When Jared passed the empty box, he saw kitten treats. He had an idea. "Mrs. Thomas, may I stay in for recess? I can get the kittens out," he said.

Jared then took the treats and crept to the radiator. He sprinkled the treats on the floor. A kitten crept out. He waited until it was eating. Then he stroked its soft fur. A paw poked out and another kitten appeared. Jared watched the kittens eat. Then he lifted both of them into the box.

He sprinkled more treats. Soon he saw two more tiny paws. Next the other kittens were eating. Jared gently put them in the box. Mrs. Thomas laid a book on the screen so they couldn't escape.

The class returned from recess. "Where were *you*?" Jessica asked.

"Class, we owe Jared a thank you. He rescued all of the kittens," Mrs. Thomas announced. Everyone cheered and applauded Jared.

"Thanks," whispered Jessica. "You're the greatest ."

Jared was so pleased that when he read, his hands didn't shake. Words didn't blur. "Jared, that was super!" said Mrs. Thomas. That day, Jared decided that third grade might not be so bad after all.

Name ______________________________ Date __________

ACTIVITY A

Directions. Fill in the box below with the time and place of the events. Then answer the question below the chart.

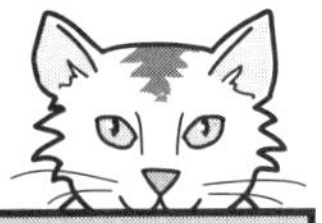

THE STORY SETTING	
When	**Where**
______________________	______________________
______________________	______________________
______________________	______________________
______________________	______________________

How is the setting important to the story as a whole? ______________

____

____

____

ACTIVITY B

Directions. Think about the three main characters in the story. Fill out the chart below to identify these characters, to describe what they are like, and to tell how they change.

Names	Personal Characteristics	Feelings and Relationships	How They Change

Name _____   Date _____

⬤ACTIVITY C

Directions. Use the main events in the story to fill out the sequence map below.

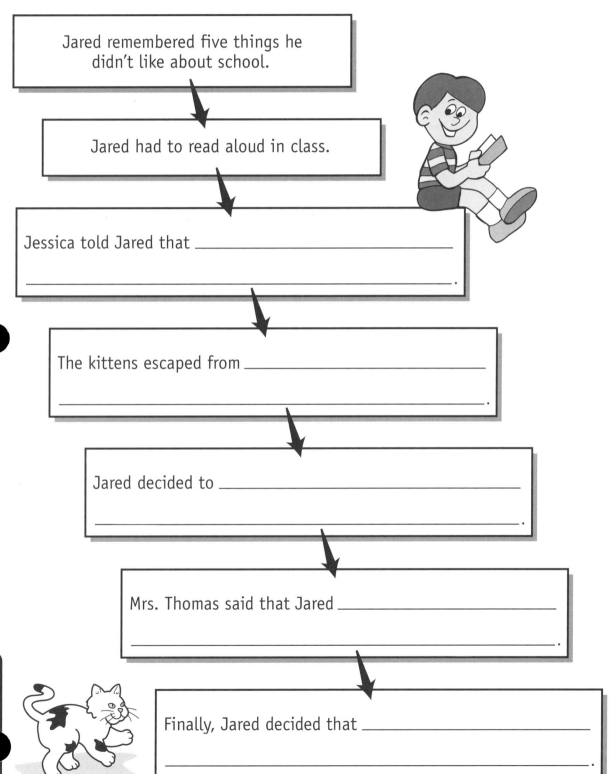

Jared remembered five things he didn't like about school.

Jared had to read aloud in class.

Jessica told Jared that _____

_____ .

The kittens escaped from _____

_____ .

Jared decided to _____

_____ .

Mrs. Thomas said that Jared _____

_____ .

Finally, Jared decided that _____

_____ .

ACTIVITY D

Directions. Answer the following two questions.

1. What is the central problem or conflict in the story?

_____

_____

_____

2. How does this problem or conflict finally get resolved?

_____

_____

_____

ACTIVITY E

Directions. Answer the following question.

★ What lesson or theme can you learn from this story?

_____

_____

_____

_____

GOING BEYOND THE READING

Directions. Read the informational article "Making a Difference." Then complete the exercises that follow.

MAKING A DIFFERENCE
by Carroll Moulton

Demetri Spiliotis was eight years old when he discovered the Growing Connection. Demetri goes to school near Miami, Florida. At the beginning of third grade, he and his classmates started to explore the problem of world hunger. The students used the Internet for their research. They found that more than one billion children and adults go to bed hungry every night. Each year, hunger and malnutrition take millions of lives.

What can be done? Demetri and the other third-graders found an international program called the Growing Connection. This program was started by the American Horticultural Society, together with the Food and Agriculture Organization (FAO) of the United Nations.

The Growing Connection gets children involved in the science of growing food. Students become directly engaged in the fight against hunger and bad health.

Every school taking part in the Growing Connection program receives six EarthBox kits. Demetri's teachers got workshop training from the program. The workshops showed the teachers how to combine plant science, information technology, and communication with different cultures.

Each EarthBox contains everything a person needs to grow delicious, healthy vegetables. For example, each box has 30 seed

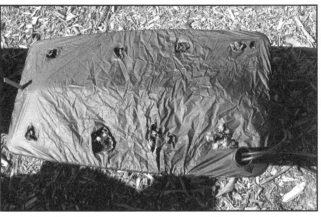

The EarthBox system uses a cover that eliminates weeding and reduces water use

packets, a bag of potting soil, fertilizer, and planting instructions. The EarthBoxes are self-contained, portable, and easy to use.

During the school year, Demetri and his classmates learned about different ways to grow food. Their work with the Growing Connection led them to a youth-run organization called Youth Can. This group uses technology to inspire, connect, and educate people about the environment all over the world. Youth Can believes that people of any age can make a difference.

Near the end of his third-grade year, Demetri was chosen to speak about the Growing Connection at a big conference of Youth Can in New York City. The conference took place at the American Museum of Natural History. Demetri and his mother Sue flew to New York.

Once there, Demetri delivered his speech. "It was a trip I will remember for a long time," says Demetri with a smile. "Making a speech in front of so many people made me a little nervous," he adds. "But it was also a great experience to show people that kids like me can make a difference."

Name _____   Date _____

● ACTIVITY A

Directions. Answer the questions below about drawing conclusions from the selection.

1. From information in the first paragraph of the article, what conclusion can you draw about the problem of world hunger?

_____

_____

2. Based on details in the article, which of the following conclusions can you most reasonably make? Circle the letter of your choice.

   A People don't have much of a chance to solve the problem of world hunger.
   B Demetri and other kids like him have shown that they can make a difference in the world.
   C The aims and goals of the Growing Connection are quite different from those of Youth Can.
   D The EarthBox kits do not work very well.

Explain your answer. _____

_____

ACTIVITY B

Directions. Based on the reading selection, answer the questions that follow about making predictions.

1. From what you have learned about Demetri Spiliotis, what kind of person do you think he will be when he grows up? Briefly explain your prediction.

_____

_____

49

2. From the details about the Growing Connection and Youth Can in the article, which prediction is the most reasonable? Circle the letter of your answer choice.

   A These organizations will have difficulty in attracting new members.

   B The organizations will have little effect on the problem of worldwide hunger.

   C These groups will have a good chance of attracting more young members in the struggle against worldwide hunger.

   D These organizations will need much more funding in order to have any hope of success.

Explain your answer. _____

_____

_____

_____

ACTIVITY C

Directions. How do the author's views influence how he describes Demetri? Circle the letter of your answer choice.

   A The author makes Demetri appear as a fun-loving and carefree young boy.

   B The author shows that Demetri plays a positive role in bringing change to the world.

   C The author suggests that Demetri is unconcerned with the problems of the world.

   D The author makes Demetri appear as nervous and awkward.

Explain your answer. _____

_____

_____

_____

A PRACTICE READING SESSION

You should mark your answers on the answer sheet on the last page of this book. When answering multiple-choice questions on the answer sheet, fill in the circle for the letter that matches your answer for each question. Use only a No. 2 pencil. You may not use a pen. When you fill in the circles, make heavy black marks. If you make a mistake, erase it completely. Make no stray marks.

*D**irections.*
Read this article. Then answer questions 1 through 6.

A HARD LESSON
by John I. White

Benjamin Franklin is remembered as an inventor, author, and signer of the Declaration of Independence. But all great people were kids once and got into trouble. In writing about his earlier life, Franklin once recalled a childhood event that he later regretted.

Franklin was born in Boston in 1706. At age ten, Ben was taken out of school to work in his father's shop. But Ben preferred playing with his friends.

The Franklins lived near the water, so Ben learned to swim and to handle small boats. He wrote that he was a leader among the boys in his neighborhood and sometimes got them into "scrapes" (*trouble*). One such time is told here in his own words:

Name _____   Date _____

"There was a salt-marsh next to the mill-pond, on the edge of which, at high water, we used to stand to fish. My idea was to build a dock for us to stand on. I showed my friends a large heap of stones meant for a new house. They would well suit our purpose. In the evening, when the workmen were gone, I brought together a number of my friends."

"Working together like so many ants, we carried the stones away to build our little dock. We were discovered. Several of us were 'corrected' (*spanked*) by our fathers.

"Though I pointed out the usefulness of the work, my father convinced me that nothing was useful that was not honest."

★★★★★★★★★★★★★★★★★★★★★★★

Read the chart below.

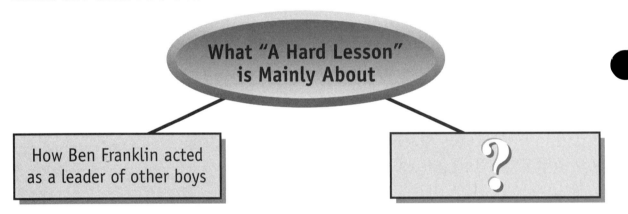

1 Which phrase **best** completes the chart?

   A what a dock is
   B how the boys worked like ants
   C what Ben Franklin learned about honesty
   D how the boys were punished by their fathers

2 According to the article, which statement is true about Ben Franklin?

   A He was taken out of school at the age of ten in order to work.
   B He never learned how to swim.
   C He found it hard to get along with other boys his age.
   D He did not learn from his experiences.

3 Read this sentence from the article.

In writing about his life, Franklin once recalled a childhood incident that he later regretted.

Based on this sentence, how did Franklin feel about the incident described in the title?

A glad
B angry
C sorry
D puzzled

4 According to the article, what was the **most** important thing Franklin learned about how to behave?

A A person's behavior should be useful.
B If you are not behaving well, do not get caught.
C A person should behave honestly.
D Some fathers are too strict with their children.

5 The author **most likely** wrote "A Hard Lesson" in order to

A tell about colonial times in Boston
B show that even Ben Franklin got into trouble
C explain how children can often work well with adults
D entertain readers with a made-up story about the past

6 One of Ben Franklin's favorite sayings was: "A lie stands on one leg, truth on two."

What message does this saying share with the story?

A It is better to act with honesty.
B A lie is often believed before the truth.
C A lie spreads faster than the truth.
D People are very willing to spread lies.

Name _____ Date _____

GRANDMA'S LOST BALANCE
by Sydney Dare

"What is the matter, grandmother dear?
   Come, let me help you. Sit down here
And rest, and I'll fan you while you tell
   How it was that you almost fell."

"I slipped a bit where the walk was wet
   And lost my balance, my little pet!"
"Lost your balance? Oh, never mind it,
   You sit still and I'll go and find it."

7 What is the poem "Grandma's Lost Balance" **mostly** about?

  A Grandma's relationship to the speaker of the poem
  B Grandma's feelings when she almost hurt herself
  C The speaker's effort to help Grandma
  D Grandma's memories of her own childhood

8 Read this line from the poem "Grandma's Lost Balance."
"And lost my balance, my little pet!"

The word "pet" in this line **most likely** means

  A animal   **C** relative
  B darling   **D** helper

9 In the poem "Grandma's Lost Balance," the poet uses the phrase "lost your balance" in order to create which of the following?

  A humor
  B a sense of sadness
  C a feeling of sympathy for Grandma
  D a sense of surprise

Name _____ Date _____

Directions.

Read this poem. Then answer questions 10 through 11.

MAY

by John Updike

Now children may
Go out of doors,
Without their coats,
To candy stores.

The apple branches
And the pear
May float their blossoms
Through the air,

And Daddy may
Get out his hoe
To plant tomatoes
In a row,

And, afterwards,
May lazily
Look at some baseball
On TV.

10 Why does the author repeat the word "may" throughout the poem?

    A to prove that May is warmer than April
    B to explain that May is in the spring
    C to show May is a month when people may do things
    D to create rhymes with other words

11 In the poem "May," which of these words **best** describes the speaker's feelings about the month of May?

    A sad   **C** happy
    B angry   **D** uncertain

D*irections.*
Read this story. Then answer questions 12 through 15.

LUCY'S PUPPY

by Kurt Daniel Lavender

"Here you go, Lucy," said Dr. Brennan. "One basset hound."

Before I could say "Thank you," my older brother, John, and his friends were on the vet's floor, playing with my bouncy baby.

"This is the puppy's family history," Dr. Brennan said, handing me the puppy's papers. "You've got a real show dog there, from a champion family. I'll go check its tests. If everything is OK, you can take the puppy home today." Dr. Brennan then turned and went back to her lab. The puppy chased after her, tripping over its long floppy ears.

"What are you going to name him?" asked Saul. "Since he comes from a champion family, we should name him after his father."

"Excuse me," I said. "It's my puppy, and I think —"

"What was his father's name?" asked Connor.

Saul grabbed the puppy's papers out of my hand before I could answer. The puppy ran after him and fell on its nose.

"The papers say his dad's name was Caesar," said Saul. "That would make our puppy Caesar the Second."

"But — I," I said.

● "I don't know," said Curtis. "He's pretty fiery. Maybe you should name him Red."

"You're right about the red part," Connor said, as the puppy chased its tail and tripped again. "But you need a stronger name for this guy. He's got a long face. How about Red Beard?"

"But—," I said.

"Or Man O' War," said Saul. "Because he runs as much as a stallion."

"Yeah, but not as well," said Curtis, laughing.

"Listen —," I said.

● They all started shouting different names at once. Just then the doctor came back. "Your puppy's tests are fine," she said. "You can take her home. Just be gentle for a couple of days. She's a little sore from all of her shots."

"Wait a minute," said John. "Her shots? She?"

"Yes," said Dr. Brennan. "Congratulations, it's a girl."

"I tried to tell you," I said. "She's a female. I think we should name her after her mother. After all, *she* was the champ in the family."

"I guess that's fair," said John.

"So what is her name?" asked Saul.

John looked at the papers and down at our puppy — she was tangled in her ears again.

"You're not going to believe it," he said. "Her name is Grace."

12 What is Lucy's **main** problem in the story?

    A to nurse her puppy back to good health
    B to deal with her brother John
    C to talk about the puppy's tests with Dr. Brennan
    D to find a good name for her new puppy

13 In the story, Saul starts out by saying that the new puppy should be named

    A after a famous race horse
    B after its mother
    C after its father
    D after Lucy

14 The chart below shows events from the story.

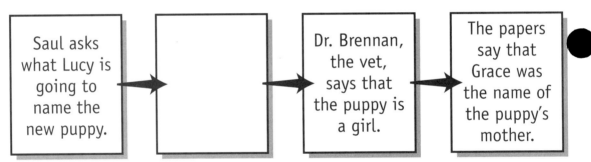

What event from the story belongs in the missing box?

    A Dr. Brennan goes back to her lab.
    B The children discuss possible names for the puppy.
    C Lucy names the puppy Grace.
    D Dr. Brennan says that there is a problem with the puppy's tests.

15 Dr. Brennan says that the puppy comes from a champion family. In this sentence, the word "champion" means

    A happy
    B large
    C prize-winning
    D colorful

Directions.

Read this story. Then answer questions 16 through 21.

CLASS PROJECT

by Carroll Moulton

Gloria lives in Buffalo, New York. Last year, her third-grade teacher was Ms. Parsons. Soon after school began, Ms. Parsons made an announcement. The whole school would have a crafts fair. All the displays for the fair had to be ready by Thanksgiving.

Gloria shook her head and raised her hand. "That doesn't give us much time," she said.

"I know, Gloria," answered Ms. Parsons. "We'll have to decide the topic for our display pretty soon."

Gloria replied, "There are lots of choices we could make."

"That's why I am going to appoint a Crafts Fair Committee," replied Ms. Parsons. "That way, the class can look into different ideas."

Soon after, Ms. Parsons appointed a committee of five students. Jamal, Luisa, Ashok and Dixon were all named to the committee. Gloria was elected chairperson. The committee had two weeks to report to the class. Then the third-graders in the class would vote on their ideas.

The committee met at Gloria's house the next afternoon. The members sat around Gloria's kitchen table. They shared their ideas. At the start of the meeting Gloria spoke up, "I think I've got a good idea. We could all make a collage for the fair."

"What's a collage?" Dixon asked.

"It's a type of art," Gloria explained. "You paste paper cutouts or other objects onto a surface like a board. A collage can tell a story in pictures. You know, like comic strips."

"Sounds neat," said Luisa. "But what story would we tell?"

"Well," said Gloria. "Look around this table. Jamal's family is from Nigeria. Dixon's grandparents came here from Canada. Luisa's family comes from Costa Rica."

"And my family is Italian American," Gloria said.

Ashok chimed in. "Don't leave me out! We Kumars are from Mumbai originally. In case you don't know, that's in India."

Gloria said, "Here's what we could do for our collage. All the objects in our collage would celebrate our roots. We could use photos, postcards, postage stamps, buttons, and other objects. And in the center we could have an American flag and a picture of the Statue of Liberty."

"Great idea!" said Jamal enthusiastically. "The Statue of Liberty has always been a symbol of freedom."

"It also stands for many different people coming together from all parts of the world," added Luisa.

"I think we have a plan to take back to Ms. Parsons," said Gloria happily. "All in favor, say Aye."

"Aye," the committee members all said together.

★★★★★★★★★★★★★★★★★★★★★★

16 According to the story, what project does Gloria's class need to plan?

A how to raise money for the soccer team uniforms
B how to increase their reading scores on tests
C how to create an exhibit for the school crafts fair
D how to elect class officers

17 According to the story, why did Ms. Parsons appoint a committee?

A She wanted to postpone the deadline for the project.
B Gloria persuaded her that this was the right thing to do.
C Ms. Parsons wanted the class to consider different ideas.
D The school rules said that a committee had to be appointed.

18 From details in the story, you can conclude that a *collage* is

A a type of art work
B any decision by a committee
C a prize awarded at a crafts fair
D a speech given by an artist

19 Read this passage from the story.

Ashok chimed in. "Don't leave me out! We Kumars are from Mumbai originally. In case you don't know, that's in India."

In these sentences, the word "originally" means

A mostly
B importantly
C in the beginning
D separately

20 The author **most likely** wrote this story to

A get readers to learn more about collages
B show that Ms. Parsons was a good decision-maker
C show how Gloria was the center of attention in the group
D show how the class committee got a good idea for their exhibit

21 According to the story, what are four items or objects that you can use in a collage? Use details from the article in your answer.

★ _____   ★ _____

★ _____   ★ _____

Name _____   Date _____

Teacher _____   Class _____●

1.	Ⓐ	Ⓑ	Ⓒ	Ⓓ
2.	Ⓐ	Ⓑ	Ⓒ	Ⓓ
3.	Ⓐ	Ⓑ	Ⓒ	Ⓓ
4.	Ⓐ	Ⓑ	Ⓒ	Ⓓ
5.	Ⓐ	Ⓑ	Ⓒ	Ⓓ
6.	Ⓐ	Ⓑ	Ⓒ	Ⓓ
7.	Ⓐ	Ⓑ	Ⓒ	Ⓓ
8.	Ⓐ	Ⓑ	Ⓒ	Ⓓ
9.	Ⓐ	Ⓑ	Ⓒ	Ⓓ
10.	Ⓐ	Ⓑ	Ⓒ	Ⓓ
11.	Ⓐ	Ⓑ	Ⓒ	Ⓓ
12.	Ⓐ	Ⓑ	Ⓒ	Ⓓ
13.	Ⓐ	Ⓑ	Ⓒ	Ⓓ
14.	Ⓐ	Ⓑ	Ⓒ	Ⓓ
15.	Ⓐ	Ⓑ	Ⓒ	Ⓓ
16.	Ⓐ	Ⓑ	Ⓒ	Ⓓ
17.	Ⓐ	Ⓑ	Ⓒ	Ⓓ
18.	Ⓐ	Ⓑ	Ⓒ	Ⓓ
19.	Ⓐ	Ⓑ	Ⓒ	Ⓓ
20.	Ⓐ	Ⓑ	Ⓒ	Ⓓ

21. ★ _____

    ★ _____

    ★ _____

    ★ _____